PRAISE FOR CAREY HARRISON

Fascinating, a superb analysis *The New York Times*

Essential reading *The Financial Times*

Bawdy, turbulent, rife with fiendish beauty *The Atlanta Journal-Constitution*

A minor miracle, the way Harrison stitches together the goonish and the gorgeous
The London Times

Breadth of vision, massive feats of scale and formal ingenuity *The Guardian*

A superb mix of slapstick, surrealism and tragedy *The Listener*

An enthralling novel, written with imaginative verve in language of strength and clarity,
recounted with masterly skill *The Irish Times*

Ambitious and fascinating, a very fine writer, exquisite in his descriptive prowess
The Irish Sunday Press

For verbal opulence and elegance of linguistic design, a wondrous thing *The Independent*

A model of judiciousness, densely packed, skillfully blended *The New York Times*

PRAISE FOR JOHN M. KELLER'S WORK

One of the most original and most brilliant of the new crop of young American fiction
writers…Reading Keller's work, one wonders if he hasn't stumbled upon the most poetic and
the most profound writer of his generation, comparable only to the South American masters,
Bolaño, Borges and Gabriel García Márquez *Roll Magazine*

Surprising, provocative, exquisitely readable, *The Box and the Briefcase* confirms Keller's
place as a significant American writer Rilla Askew, author of *Fire in Beulah*

He has written the city's poverty and gore in bold colors and cold gales of anger…Hop on
board for *Know Your Baker* Charles Bowden, author of *Blues for Cannibals*

Keller's novel delivers…He takes our current-day media obsession with physical perfection
and projects a near future in which these tendencies have reached their logical, dreadful
extreme…A page-turner. *World Literature Today*

Where Did You Get That Bitch?

The Basic Grammar They've
Stopped Teaching You

———

By Carey Harrison and John M. Keller

Illustrations and Cover Photography by Claire Lambe

www.drcicerobooks.com
www.careyharrison.net   www.knowyourbaker.com

Cover models: Chiara Harrison Lambe
and Emmeline Loubeau

Dr. Cicero Books
New York Rio de Janeiro Paris
First Edition
Manufactured in the United States of América

ISBN: 0692277862
ISBN-13: 978-0692277867

For our students

Table of Contents

Part One: The Comma

Part Two: Other Punctuation

Appendix

Preface

Where do commas go?

Where you breathe, you say.

Where else? Between items in a list. Anywhere else? Is that it?

How often do you breathe? And when?

It seems that, in the last twenty years, teachers have stopped teaching grammar. Perhaps they thought students couldn't learn it, or didn't need to.

All around the country, people who haven't been taught grammar are throwing commas into sentences without thinking twice, or else avoiding them.

"Where did you get that bitch?" Or is it, "Where did you get that, bitch?"

Introduction

Where did you get that bitch?
Is that what you mean? Does this question have something to do with a dog?

Or do you mean:
Where did you get that, bitch?
Are you calling someone a bitch?
If so, this is the Comma of Direct Address.

Eddie, my friend is dead.
Does this mean that Eddie, your friend, is dead? Or are you telling Eddie that your friend is dead?
If you're saying that your friend, Eddie, is dead, the line should read:
Eddie, my friend, is dead.
This is the Stepping-Away (and Stepping-Back) Comma.

Here's what can happen if you don't put a comma in a place where it **must** go:
Because he ate the man on the bus with the striped shirt was happy.

Here's what can happen if you put a comma in a place where it **must not** go:
White people, who are racists, often use racial slurs.
Did you mean to say that all white people are racists?
If so, this is perfectly good grammar.
Did you mean to say that all white people use racial slurs?
If so, this is perfectly good grammar.
But if you meant that those white people who are racists tend to use racial slurs, then your sentence should look like this:

White people who are racists often use racial slurs.

While teaching grammar in the classroom, we developed a new, simpler way for students to understand grammar.

What follows is our new approach.

Part One: The Comma

Chapter One

The Comma of Direct Address

1.

The Comma of Direct Address is used when directly addressing someone or something.

Don't be rude, Megan.
Megan, don't be rude.
Hello, Keith.
Goodbye, Doctor.
Do you want to go with us, Britney?
Farewell, New York.
Damn you, printer!
Honey, do you love me?
Hey, Sasha, would you take a look at this?
Listen, Mr. Know-It-All, I've got a problem with you.

Here's what can happen if you don't put in the Comma of Direct Address:

Please eat Aunt Linda!

How about:
You are his honey.

Or did you mean:
You are his, honey.

One more. Two sentences, meaning different things:

Are you David?
Are you, David?

EXERCISE 1:

Put in the Commas of Direct Address in the sentences below. How many of the sentences below would also work *without* a comma?

1.) *Melissa are you listening?*

2.) *I want to know God.*

3.) *Happy Birthday Mr. President.*

4.) *Let me be Romeo.*

5.) *Oh Pops I feel terrible!*

6.) *You're mad precious.*

7.) *Why not Harry?*

Chapter Two

The Stepping-Away (and Stepping-Back) Comma

1.

The Stepping-Away Comma interrupts a sentence or part of a sentence to add information.

I need coffee, a drink invented in Ethiopia.

The Stepping-Back Comma brings you back to where you were before the interruption.

I need coffee, a drink invented in Ethiopia, when I get up in the morning.

The Stepping-Away Comma shows that you are *stepping away* from the sentence in progress to offer additional information. The Stepping-Back Comma allows you to pick up right where you left off.

, a drink invented in Ethiopia,

I need coffee   *when I get up in the morning.*

Here are a few other examples:

His last name, which is of Greek origin, is Stephanopoulos.
He went to Jamaica, where hip hop was born.
I met my girlfriend, who wears glasses, at work.
It's dangerous to carry around scissors, which are sharp objects.

EXERCISE 1:

Punctuate the following:

The United States which is composed of 50 states is just south of Canada.

The United States which is just south of Canada is composed of 50 states.

Bugs Bunny who was born in 1938 is the oldest living rabbit in America.

The Mona Lisa a famous painting was not painted by my brother-in-law.

We went to Brooklyn a city famous for its lack of hotels and couldn't find anywhere to stay.

Did you put in *both* the Stepping-Away Comma *and* the Stepping-Back Comma?

EXERCISE 2:

Combine the following sentences using Stepping-Away and Stepping-Back Commas:

Example: *Austin is the capital of Texas. Austin is the live-music capital of the United States.*

Any of the following is correct:
Austin, which is the live-music capital of the United States, is the capital of Texas.
OR:
Austin, the live-music capital of the United States, is the capital of Texas.
OR:
Austin, which is the capital of Texas, is the live-music capital of the United States.
OR:
Austin, the capital of Texas, is the live-music capital of the United States.

As in the examples, please feel free to add words such as "who" and "which" after the Stepping-Away Comma. You will also need to remove some words.

First, please review the four examples at the bottom of the previous page.

1.) Cows are bizarre animals. They can be tipped over while they are sleeping.

2.) Cycling is a demanding sport. Cycling has recently become controversial because of drug use.

3.) The senator has been convicted of grand theft auto. He is 78 years old.

4.) Elvis is believed to still be alive. It is said that he lives in the basement at Graceland, which has recently been refurbished.

2.

Which vs. that:

"Which" is a useful word for stepping away.

The United States, which is just south of Canada, is composed of 50 states.
This is the last time you'll see me dive into freezing water, which is not fun at all.
The Dodgers' outfield, which is full of holes, is a disgrace.
Coffee, which is from Ethiopia, can be expensive.

When using "which" to step-away, always use a comma before "which."

Here's when you use "that" instead of "which":

Coffee that is from Ethiopia can be expensive.
Coffee, which is from Ethiopia, can be expensive.

The first sentence tells us that Ethiopian coffee—unlike other coffees—can be expensive.
The second sentence tells us two things: coffee comes from Ethiopia, and it can be expensive.

Indian food, which I like, can sometimes make me sick.
Indian food that I like can sometimes make me sick.

That was my first date, which went well.
That was my first date that went well.

I need money, which is odd because I'm rich.
I need money that is odd because I'm rich.

Note: if you replace the word "which" with "that" in the sentences above, a comma is not used. Here are a few more examples:

The book that I read last night was full of true crimes of passion.
Last night I saw a dog that I wanted to steal and take home for myself.
This is the basketball that I used to shoot my first basket.
The thing that I love about her is her teeth.

3.

Now let's look at how Stepping-Away and Stepping-Back Commas can change the meaning of the sentence.

Women, who are seven foot tall, have a hard time getting dates.

Is this correct? Did you mean to say that *all* women are seven foot tall? If not, and if you mean that seven-foot-tall women in particular have a hard time getting dates, this should read:

Women who are seven foot tall have a hard time getting dates.

Try this one. See if you can spot the difference in meaning between:

Guys, who rob stores, should be arrested.
and
Guys who rob stores should be arrested.

In the first example, *Guys, who rob stores, should be arrested,* the comma steps away after "guys." What follows the comma, the additional information, defines **in general** what the word or phrase before the comma means. The first example suggests that all guys rob stores. It also suggests that all guys should be arrested.

If you write, as in the second example, *Guys who rob stores should be arrested* (without any commas), you will be defining *which* kinds of guy **in particular** you are talking about. In other words, *guys who rob stores.*

What if you wanted to say that New Jersey teachers are smarter than the rest? Would you write:

Teachers, who are from New Jersey, are smarter than the rest.
or
Teachers who are from New Jersey are smarter than the rest.

The first sentence suggests that *all* teachers are from New Jersey, which is definitely not true.

The Stepping-Away Comma can really help us to prevent confusion:

Find out who Gandhi was and why he died in the next five minutes.

Clearly, this needs a comma. (You might be better off re-writing the sentence completely.)

What about this one:

I found Melissa a dance teacher.

This means you found a dance teacher for Melissa.

If you really meant that Melissa is a dance teacher, and you found her, you need the Stepping-Away Comma.

I found Melissa, a dance teacher.
Or you could write:
I found Melissa, who is a dance teacher.

See if you can tell the difference between:

I gave the money to the beggar who needed it.
I gave the money to the beggar, who needed it.

Both are correct. But they mean different things.

The first sentence means that I gave money only to the beggar who needed it. The second sentence tells us that the beggar I gave money to needed it.

EXERCISE 3 (answers at the end of the chapter):

1.) Americans, who are multi-millionaires, can afford a private jet.
Americans who are multi-millionaires can afford a private jet.

Which of the two sentences says that all Americans are multi-millionaires and can afford a private jet?

2.) *Women who have long beards are highly prized in circuses.*
Women, who have long beards, are highly prized in circuses.

Which of the two sentences says that only those women who have long beards are highly prized in circuses?

3.) *Alicia will take one last subway trip to the airport.*
Alicia will take one last subway trip, to the airport.

Which sentence says that Alicia's trip to the airport will be her last subway trip ever?

4.) *My brother who plays the guitar is a genius.*
My brother, who plays the guitar, is a genius.

Which of these is correct?

5.) *Eddie, my friend is dead.*
Eddie, my friend, is dead.

In which sentence is Eddie dead?

4.

As we said at the beginning of this chapter, Stepping-Away and Stepping-Back Commas interrupt a sentence or part of a sentence to add information—lots of different types of information. There are also lots of types of interruptions.

Here are some:

She was he thought a great girl.
When he wondered would the train arrive?
Every time you see her like I said she is going to ask you for money.
I for example am not dating anyone right now.
His toes on the other hand were fine.

These sentences should read:

She was, he thought, a great girl.
When, he wondered, would the train arrive?
Every time you see her, like I said, she is going to ask you for money.
I, for example, am not dating anyone right now.
His toes, on the other hand, were fine.

Some interruptions are very brief:

He was sure, however, that he was being followed.
Winter, I told him, is my favorite time of year.

Others are longer:

The supermodel, having decided that she would retire from the catwalk as soon as she reached the age of 22 so that she could pursue a career as an actor, went to her first acting class on Tuesday.

EXERCISE 4:

Place the missing Stepping-Away and Stepping-Back Commas where they belong in the following:

1.) He fell without thinking into a ditch.

2.) He said that despite her appetite for strange foods he was attracted to her.

3.) Even though he likes her knowing that she doesn't eat dairy he served milk.

4.) Henry's grandfather has lived to the age of 108 and even though he is proud of his great age he wakes up every morning and says loudly for all those to hear, "Not again!"

5.) He knew that for example he wouldn't be able to wash dishes with a broken wrist.

6.) By the power vested in me by the state of Georgia despite my desire not to offend anyone I am required to arrest litterbugs.

7.) Medically speaking when somebody runs four miles over rough country they will be tired.

8.) In the second sentence thanks to the Stepping-Back Comma "my friend" defines Eddie.

9.) He said it was his brother dead for many years now who had started the fire.

10.) He found the ring as I mentioned in the street.

For #10, which did you choose:

He found the ring, as I mentioned, in the street.
Or:
He found the ring, as I mentioned in the street.

Clearly, these two sentences have completely different meanings.

6.

Changing the order of information in a sentence, using Stepping-Away and Stepping-Back Commas, can make certain parts of the sentence stand out.

For example:

I told him winter was my favorite time of year.
Winter, I told him, is my favorite time of year.

The second example requires Stepping-Away and Stepping-Back Commas. Notice where the first comma goes: right before we step away (right before the information we moved).

Here are some more examples:

Having decided that she would retire from the catwalk as soon as she reached the age of 22 so that she could pursue a career as an actor, the supermodel went to her first acting class on Tuesday.

The supermodel, having decided that she would retire from the catwalk as soon as she reached the age of 22 so that she could pursue a career as an actor, went to her first acting class on Tuesday.

I mean, he said he was sober.
He said he was, I mean, sober.

After all, he was a good man.
He was, after all, a good man.

However, I am pretty happy.
I am, however, pretty happy.

To my surprise, I remembered it the next day.
I remembered it, to my surprise, the next day.

I imagined he'd be dead by midnight.
He'd be dead, I imagined, by midnight.

The way I see it, he was an idiot.
He was, the way I see it, an idiot.

Here's an example where changing the order of information also changes the emphasis—or mood—of the sentence:

For example, I am not dating anyone right now.
I, for example, am not dating anyone right now.

The first one might follow something along the lines of: I'm so busy that I don't have time for anything. *For example, I am not dating anyone right now.*

The second one might follow something like: Just because you're single doesn't mean you're a loser. *I, for example, am not dating anyone right now.*

7.

Sentences using Stepping-Away and Stepping-Back Commas must still be complete sentences if you remove the additional information (along with the commas):

He was, the way I see it, an idiot.

If we take out the additional information, "the way I see it," this is still a complete sentence:

He was an idiot.

The same goes for this one:

The supermodel, having decided that she would retire from the catwalk as soon as she reached the age of 22 so that she could pursue a career as an actor, went to her first acting class on Tuesday.

The supermodel went to her first acting class on Tuesday.

Now take the following:

I came to school, and because of lack of coffee and my usual bagel, I fell asleep.

This is incorrect.

As we said before, sentences using Stepping-Away and Stepping-Back Commas must still be complete sentences if you remove the additional information.

Without the additional information—what comes *after* the Stepping-Away Comma and *before* the Stepping-Back Comma (along with the commas themselves)—you would be left with:

I came to school I fell asleep.

This is a Run-On. We will discuss Run-Ons and how to avoid them in Chapter Four.

So then how would you punctuate this sentence correctly?

You place the comma *after* "and."

Like this:

I came to school and, because of a lack of coffee and my usual bagel, I fell asleep.

So that, if you remove the additional information —

    , because of lack of coffee and my usual bagel,
I came to school and   *I fell asleep*

You are left with:

I came to school and I fell asleep.

This is a complete sentence.
(Note: In another chapter, we will discuss whether or not to use a comma before "and" in such cases.)

Here's another example:

He came to school with a headache, yet despite the fact that it was causing him a great deal of pain, he forgot all about it when he saw Tasha.

This would be the same as writing:
He came to school with a headache he forgot all about it when he saw Tasha.

In this case, we have two complete sentences, jammed together, without correct punctuation.

CORRECT: *He came to school with a headache yet, despite the fact that it was causing him a great deal of pain, he forgot all about it when he saw Tasha.*

This would be the same as writing:
He came to school with a headache yet he forgot all about it when he saw Tasha.

This is a complete sentence.

EXERCISE 5 (answers at the end of the chapter):

Place the missing Stepping-Away and Stepping-Back Commas where they belong in the following:

1.) Enrique is in love with Janice but because she doesn't love him he doesn't plan to ask her out.

2.) Janice could never love Enrique but even though he won't stop following her around she'll never tell him to go away.

3.) Janice came to school exhausted and after she had finished half a sandwich she fell asleep.

4.) Enrique saw Janice and seeing her asleep carefully bagged the contents of Janice's uneaten lunch and stored it for future use.

5.) Jason has been stalking Enrique and Janice but sadly does not realize they are not together.

6.) Janice would definitely go out with Jason yet because she has never met him this is not yet in their cards.

7.) But this will never be in their cards because despite the fact that she will eventually meet him she will discover that Jason is head over heels in love with Enrique.

Is it possible to have a comma before the "and" *and* after the "and"?—as in the following example:

I came to school, and, because of lack of coffee and my usual bagel, I fell asleep.

Yes, it is also correct—but less common.

The first comma is a Comma of Equal Weight, which will be discussed in detail in Chapter Four.

———

EXERCISE 3 ANSWERS:

1.) It's the first one. Remember: the comma tells us that we are Stepping-Away from the word before the comma to define *in general* what that word means. The second sentence, *Americans who are multi-millionaires can afford a private jet,* which doesn't have any commas, describes a *particular* type of American: those who are multi-millionaires.

2.) It's also the first one. The first sentence tells us which women in particular are highly prized in circuses—women with long beards. The second sentence suggests that women in general have long beards. It also suggests that women in general are highly prized in circuses.

3.) The second one.

4.) Both are correct, but they suggest different things. The first sentence suggests that the speaker is distinguishing among his brothers. The one who plays the guitar is a genius. The second sentence suggests that the speaker has one brother. This brother is a genius. He also happens to play the guitar.

5.) The second one. In the second one, the Stepping-Away and Stepping-Back Commas allow you to explain who Eddie is—your friend—and what he is: dead. The first sentence is also correct, but means something different. In the first sentence, the comma is the Comma of Direct Address, which was explained in Chapter One. In the first sentence, the speaker is addressing Eddie, explaining that his or her friend, whose name we do not know, is dead.

EXERCISE 5 ANSWERS:

1.) Enrique is in love with Janice but, because she doesn't love him, he doesn't plan to ask her out.

2.) Janice could never love Enrique but, even though he won't stop following her around, she'll never tell him to go away.

3.) Janice came to school exhausted and, after she had finished half a sandwich, she fell asleep.

4.) Enrique saw Janice and, seeing her asleep, carefully bagged the contents of Janice's uneaten lunch and stored it for future use.

5.) Jason has been stalking Enrique and Janice but, sadly, does not realize they are not together.

6.) Janice would definitely go out with Jason yet, because she has never met him, this is not yet in their cards.

7.) But this will never be in their cards because, despite the fact that she will eventually meet him, she will discover that Jason is head over heels in love with Enrique.

Chapter Three

Introductory Commas

Here are some examples of how introductory commas are used:

Waiting for the bus, he used his cell phone.
If you leave me, I won't come back.
Oh my God, I left the gas on.
Doing time for Grand Theft Auto, Howard played the market successfully.
His task finished, Abe went back to his trailer home.

Here's what can sometimes happen if you leave out the Introductory Comma:

Because he ate the man on the bus with the white shirt was happy.
After he showered the girl with the dragon tattoo gave him a kiss and left.

A comma will clear up the confusion:

Because he ate, the man on the bus with the white shirt was happy.
After he showered, the girl with the dragon tattoo gave him a kiss and left.

1.

Introductory Commas After Prepositional Phrases

Prepositions are words that locate other words in time or space. They indicate direction, location, time and possession.

Direction: *toward* the tree, *from* the terrace, *through* the looking glass

Location: *to* the lighthouse, *under* the volcano, *between* us, *out of* Africa

Time: *after* dark, *before* sunset, *between* the acts, *around* midnight, *as* I lay dying

Possession: *of* our time, *of* the United States, *without* a sigh, *with* child

The prepositional phrase includes the preposition **and** the words that complete it:

toward the tree

from the terrace

through the looking glass

When you have one Prepositional Phrase at the **beginning** of the sentence, you **may** put a comma **after** the Prepositional Phrase, if you choose to:

From the terrace, I watched them play.

From the terrace I watched them play.

Both are correct. The first uses a comma for dramatic emphasis to make the reader more aware of the location.

When you have **more than one** Prepositional Phrase at the beginning of the sentence, you **must** put a comma after the final Prepositional Phrase:

In the streets around the freeway, you can hear the traffic.

In the streets around Lake Shore Drive in Chicago, you can hear the traffic.

In the middle of the night, a bird sang.

In the middle of the night by my window, a bird sang.

In the middle of the night by my window in Egypt, a bird sang.

2.

Introductory Commas After Adverbs

Adverbs describe verbs, adjectives and other adverbs, answering the question, "how?":

rapidly

suddenly

dramatically

overwhelmingly

somewhat

extremely

When you have an adverb at the beginning of the sentence, you **may** follow it with a comma for dramatic emphasis or different shades of meaning:

Rapidly, the noise faded.

Suddenly, he croaked.

Suddenly he croaked.

Unfortunately, he lost control of the wheel.

Overwhelmingly, the students voted for Pedro.

Overwhelmingly the students voted for Pedro.

Dramatically, the sky darkened.

Soon, the sky darkened.

Is there a difference in shade of meaning between:

Gradually, the noise faded.

Gradually the noise faded.

If you use the Introductory Comma, the noise doesn't seem to fade as gradually as it does without the comma.

Do you agree?

3.

Independent Elements

An Independent Element is a word or phrase that does not add any new information to a sentence. It is often used as extra emphasis or as a habit of speech:

you know
like
by the way
anyway
yes
no
oh
I mean

When you have an Independent Element at the **beginning** of the sentence, always put a comma **after** the Independent Element:

You know, he's great.
Yes, he's great.

Here's what can sometimes happen if you don't put in the Introductory Comma after an Independent Element. Suppose you wrote:

You know he's great.

This would be the same as saying: *You know **that** he's great.*

You know, he's great, however—with a comma—is simply a way of introducing *He's great.*

You could also say it:

He's great, you know (which uses a Stepping-Away Comma)
or even:
He's, you know, great (which uses a Stepping-Away and a Stepping-Back Comma)

As you can see, Independent Elements can be moved to different parts of sentences and are **always** separated by commas.

For example:
Like, he's awesome. (Introductory Comma)
He's, like, awesome. (Stepping-Away and Stepping-Back Commas)
Right, he's, like, awesome. (Introductory Comma **and** Stepping-Away and Stepping-Back Commas)
He's, like, awesome, right? (Stepping-Away and Stepping-Back Commas **and** another Stepping-Away Comma)

EXERCISE 1:

Name these commas:

1.) Oh, what were you going to say? _____

2.) I told him that, no, I wouldn't go out with him. _____

3.) Huh, did you really say that? _____

4.) Yeah, he was, I mean, really pissed. _____

5.) I bet you were, like, out of there. _____

4.

Interjections

Interjections are exclamations. On their own, they would be punctuated with exclamation points:

Wow!

Oh!

Oh my God!

Darn!

Argh!

Hot damn!

Oops!

Note: A key difference between Independent Elements and Interjections is that Interjections can be used on their own with exclamations points, as above.

Find some more of your own.

When you have an Interjection at the **beginning** of the sentence, always put an Introductory Comma **after** the Interjection:

Damn, you're looking good.

Phew, I nearly dropped it.

Holy crap, you're alive.

Just as with Independent Elements, Interjections can be moved to different parts of sentences and are **always** separated by commas:

I thought, hmm, she's crazier than I thought she was.
She's, like, ouch, who the hell are you?
Batman went, holy sheepshit, I'm out of here.

5.

When you have an incomplete sentence followed by a complete sentence, a comma is **always** used.

What is a complete sentence?

Some are short:

I laughed.
Mercy always cried.
The young student yawned for all to see.

Some are longer:

On Friday the student with the highest grades in the class was honored for her ground-breaking paper on the use of the Stepping-Away and Stepping-Back Comma.

These are **not** complete sentences:

Although I laughed
Even if Mercy always cried
After the young student yawned for all to see
Because on Friday the student with the highest grades in the class was honored for her ground-breaking paper on the use of the Stepping-Away and Stepping-Back Comma

Why are they not complete sentences?

This is because using a word or phrase like "when," "although," or "after" creates an incomplete sentence. An incomplete sentence always needs to be followed by an Introductory Comma and then a complete sentence:

Although I laughed, Mercy cried.
Even if Mercy always cried, she was overall a pretty happy person.

Examples of such words or phrases used to begin incomplete sentences include:

although, as, as soon as, because, before, by the time, despite, even if, even though, every time, if, in case, in the event that, just in case, now that, once, only if, since, the first time, though, unless, until, whenever, whereas, whether or not, while.

As we said at the beginning of this section, when you have an incomplete sentence followed by a complete sentence, a comma is **always** used.

EXERCISE 2:

Punctuate the following:

1.) While he smoked his wife was planning his downfall.

2.) Because she was tired the young student yawned for all to see.

3.) When he cried Mercy always laughed.

4.) If you leave me I won't come back.

5.) When I reached six feet tall I changed my hairstyle.

6.) Upon entering the room I saw him sitting there.

If you wrote the same sentences **in reverse order**—with the complete sentence first—a comma is no longer necessary:

His wife was planning his downfall while he smoked
I won't come back if you leave me.
I changed my hairstyle when I reached six feet tall.

A comma is no longer necessary, but you could use one (a Stepping-Away Comma), depending on the intended effect.

Compare:
I changed my hairstyle when I reached six feet tall.
I changed my hairstyle, when I reached six feet tall.

Is there a difference in emphasis?

The sentences still mean the same thing. However, in the first example, you might argue that the emphasis is on *when* I changed my hairstyle. In other words, you are suggesting there's a connection between reaching six feet tall and changing your hairstyle. In the second example, you might argue that the emphasis is on the *fact* that I changed hairstyles, which I did when I reached six feet tall. (The Stepping-Away Comma makes reaching six-foot-tall **additional** information, rather than **essential** information.)

EXERCISE 3:

Punctuate the following (if necessary), noting which comes first, the complete or incomplete sentence:

1.) When she was hypnotized she got pretty crazy.

2.) She got pretty crazy when she was hypnotized.

3.) After I visited the murderer went on a rampage.

4.) The murderer went on a rampage after I visited.

5.) Alex made a lot of money even though he had no use for it.

6.) Because he vomited his lunch looked more attractive.

7.) Even though he was so athletic he was always sick.

8.) Lakisha has been an exceptional writer since she was born.

9.) Now that I'm 21 I'm leaving home.

10.) I will bring you $100 as soon as I can.

Here's one more exercise, this time using all the different types of introductory material:

EXERCISE 4 :
Punctuate the following:

1.) Walking through the park she whistled.

2.) Wherever you want to go your shadow goes with you.

3.) Eaten up by mosquitoes she swore to wear twice as many clothes next time.

4.) Singing his favorite song too loudly on the subway he got a lot of angry looks.

5.) Yo I ain't yo' bitch no more.

6.) Lightly carefully he drew back the curtain.

7.) At the end of the day she said she was bored.

8.) Eating pizza he sneered at the passers-by.

9.) Whatever I'm going to go anyway.

10.) However I didn't go.

11.) Her hair finally done after six hours at the salon she came out a redhead.

12.) Walked by her owner Rosie ignored the attentions of other dogs.

7.

To summarize:

When you use Stepping-Away and Stepping-Back Commas, you interrupt the sentence to add information:

The professor, having spoken for an hour about grammar, asked for a break.
I, for example, am not dating anyone right now.

If you introduced this information at the beginning of the sentence, you would use an introductory comma:

Having spoken for an hour about grammar, the professor asked for a break.
For example, I am not dating anyone right now.

As you can see, Introductory Commas are used when the additional information is placed at the **beginning** of the sentence, and Stepping-Away and Stepping-Back Commas are used when additional information is added in the **middle** of the sentence.

———

EXERCISE 3 ANSWERS:

1.) When she was hypnotized, she got pretty crazy. INCOMPLETE→COMPLETE

2.) She got pretty crazy when she was hypnotized. COMPLETE→INCOMPLETE
OR: She got pretty crazy, when she was hypnotized. (The Stepping-Away Comma is optional.)

3.) After I visited, the murderer went on a rampage. INCOMPLETE→COMPLETE

4.) The murderer went on a rampage after I visited. COMPLETE→INCOMPLETE
OR: The murderer went on a rampage, after I visited. (The Stepping-Away Comma is optional.)

5.) Alex made a lot of money even though he had no use for it.
COMPLETE→INCOMPLETE
OR: Alex made a lot of money, even though he had no use for it. (The Stepping-Away Comma is optional.)

6.) Because he vomited, his lunch looked more attractive. INCOMPLETE→COMPLETE

7.) Even though he was so athletic, he was always sick. INCOMPLETE→COMPLETE

8.) Lakisha has been an exceptional writer since she was born. COMPLETE→INCOMPLETE
OR: Lakisha has been an exceptional writer, since she was born. (The Stepping-Away Comma is optional.)

9.) Now that I'm 21, I'm leaving home. INCOMPLETE→COMPLETE

10.) I will bring you $100 as soon as I can. COMPLETE→INCOMPLETE
OR: I will bring you $100, as soon as I can. (The Stepping-Away Comma is optional.)

Chapter Four

The Comma of Equal Weight

There are three different ways in which The Comma of Equal Weight is used:

1.

The Comma of Equal Weight separates items in a list:

Harry sang, danced, laughed, and played the ukulele.

I bought cucumbers, cookies, coffee, and a copy of the Lagos Times.

I dislike the following: noisy kids, bloody noses, people who think they're better than you because they've got a car, and mint tea.

Each item in the list is divided into **equal** units by commas.

A lot of people want to know whether to include a comma before the final item in the list. Sometimes, a final comma helps to make it clear that the two final items in the list are in fact separate:

There are always stories in my newspaper about local burglaries, car accidents, the mayor, and sexual misconduct.

(Unless you were talking about the mayor's sexual misconduct...)

If there's no confusion, then you can leave the comma out:

I bought cucumbers, cookies, coffee and a copy of the Lagos Times.

2.

The Comma of Equal Weight is used between adjectives:

The blue, red and green fish swam around the bowl.

These adjectives all belong to the same category: colors.

The athletes turned out to be Christian, Muslim, Buddhist, and agnostic.

These adjectives all belong to the same category: religion.

If the adjectives belong to different categories, a comma is not used:

The hungry triangular blue fish swam around the bowl.
The intelligent Italian man asked for seconds.

Note the order of the adjectives. You wouldn't write:

the Italian intelligent man

This is because adjectives are ordered by category, with certain categories nearest to the noun (in the phrase above, the word "man").

It seems that, over time, certain categories of adjectives have acquired a greater or lesser ranking:

Species outranks religion
a Catholic human being

Religion outranks nationality

an American Catholic human being

Nationality outranks race

a black American Catholic human being

Nationality also outranks material

a cotton Italian sweater

Material outranks color

a red cotton Italian sweater

Color outranks Shape

A rectangular black box

Color also outranks Human/Animal Age

an elderly black American Catholic human being

Human/Animal Age outranks Other Characteristics:

An elderly golden Italian cocker spaniel dog.

More examples of each rank, from highest to lowest:

SPECIES: human, feline, hominid, avian

RELIGION: Muslim, Christian, atheist, agnostic, Hindu

NATIONALITY: Pakistani, Australian, Kurdish, Neapolitan

RACE: Hispanic, black, Pacific Islander, Caucasian

MATERIAL: cotton, wooden, metal, silk

COLOR: black, green, turquoise, scarlet, dark

SHAPE: rectangular, trapezoidal, square, circular

HUMAN/ANIMAL AGE: 17-year-old, young, elderly, septuagenarian

OTHER CHARACTERISTICS: large, fat, ugly, clever, frustrating, depressed, overwhelmed, studious, prideful, awesome, sweet, incapable, computer-generated, overweight, tall, skinny, isolated, cute, cool, unexpected, idiotic, lovable

In other words:

When an adjective is of a higher category than the one(s) before it, no commas are used:
the skinny old blond Italian Buddhist

However, if you are using two adjectives of equal rank, you put a comma between the adjectives of equal rank:

a tall, ugly stranger
the happy, overweight, overfed spaniel
the drunk, educated, suspicious dude

Some sentences combine adjectives of equal rank with adjectives of unequal rank:

a clever, isolated, skeptical, bitter young red-headed Peruvian intellectual
the vicious, underfed, over-trained Antarctic sea lion
an eager, determined, tremendously uneducated, clairvoyant United States senator
a large, fat, ugly, clever, frustrating, depressed, overwhelmed, studious, prideful, awesome, sweet, incapable, computer-generated, overweight, tall, skinny, isolated, cute, cool, unexpected, idiotic, lovable septuagenarian Pacific Islander Hindu

EXERCISE 1:
Punctuate the following:

1.) The strong faithful dog was a strong and faithful dog.

2.) The tall Italian stranger was a tall dark stranger.

3.) The heavy blue blanket was a heavy expensive blanket.

4.) The terrible cruel rule felt like a terrible cruel punishment.

5.) The kind old lady gave me a soft disgusting cookie.

6.) The kind old lady gave me a big old hug.

Note:

Some adjectives go right before the noun because of their regular use together:

the unexpected cold front

fatal friendly fire

boot-cut, pre-shrunk skinny jeans

good old boy

big old hug

As this "ranking" system has evolved over time, there will be plenty of exceptions in everyday use. When in doubt, apply the rules above.

3.

The Comma of Equal Weight also allows you to combine two complete sentences.

What is a complete sentence? We discussed complete and incomplete sentences in Chapter Three on page 43.

Here's an example of an incomplete sentence followed by a complete sentence. As we said in Chapter Three, this requires an Introductory Comma:

While I cried, the student laughed.

Suppose you wanted to write the same sentence without using "while." That would give you two complete sentences:

I cried. The student laughed.

What if you wanted to join them with a comma?

You would use the Comma of Equal Weight. However, the Comma of Equal Weight **must always** be followed by one of these seven words: *and, but, or, for, nor, so* or *yet.*

I cried, and the student laughed.
I cried, but the student laughed.
I cried, so the student laughed.
I cried, for the student laughed.
I cried, yet the student laughed.
I cried, or I appeared to do so.
I didn't cry, nor did the student laugh.

In each of these examples, note that there is a complete sentence *before* the Comma of Equal Weight **and** *after* the Comma of Equal Weight and *and, but, or, for, nor, so* or *yet.*

("Nor" is an exception. Notice how in the final example, the word "nor" causes some of the words in the second part of the sentence to change order. But we would still have a complete sentence if you put it in the usual order: *The student did laugh.*)

A lot of people write:

I laughed, the student cried.

But this is incorrect.

Why? This is because—as we said above—when combining complete sentences, the Comma of Equal Weight **must always** be followed by one of these seven words: *and, but, or, for, nor, so* or *yet.*

EXERCISE 2.

Combine the following sentences using a Comma of Equal Weight with one of the seven words (and, but, or, for, nor, so, yet) for each example, and punctuate the sentence correctly:

Example: *I like you. You like me.*
One possible answer: *I like you, **and** you like me.*

1.) Jeremiah really likes his girlfriend. He is going to buy her a book on grammar.

2.) Jeremiah's girlfriend has buck teeth. He really likes her.

3.) Jeremiah doesn't have any money. He really would like to buy a house.

4.

Be careful. When using the Comma of Equal Weight to combine sentences, you **must** have complete sentences on both sides of the comma.

Here are some examples of sentences that contain only one complete sentence and therefore do not use a Comma of Equal Weight:

I wanted to go to the game but couldn't really afford it.

"I wanted to go to the game" is a complete sentence.
"But couldn't really afford it" is not.

The student cried or seemed to do so.

"The student cried" is a complete sentence.
"or seemed to do so" is not.

I am tall but happy.
"I am tall" is a complete sentence.
"but happy" is not.

In each of the above cases, you **could** use a comma—a Stepping-Away Comma—depending on the intended effect:

I wanted to go to the game, but couldn't really afford it.
The student cried, or seemed to do so.
I am tall, but happy.

A comma is not necessary in any of the above cases.

However, if you wanted to use a Comma of Equal Weight, you would need to **add** words so that there are complete sentences on each side of the comma:

I wanted to go to the game, but I couldn't really afford it.
The student cried, or he seemed to do so.

I am tall, but I am happy.

EXERCISE 3.

Here are some sentences, not all of which require commas. If you add a comma, identify it as either a Comma of Equal Weight or a Stepping-Away Comma.:

I went to the airport and had a strange experience. The customs official pulled me aside and he told me to come with him. I didn't want to go but I had no choice for he was the authority there. I followed him into a room and saw a whole lot of sad-looking individuals. I asked him what this place was but he wouldn't answer my question nor did he say anything at all. This freaked me out but I kept my cool. I asked one of the others if she knew what we were doing here and she stared at me blankly. I wanted to know if she spoke English but I didn't know in what language to ask her. We sat there for an hour or was it longer? No one came nor did any of my companions speak yet I felt strangely calm.

5.

Run-Ons

It seems that, perhaps because of its name, many people think Run-On sentences are sentences that go on for too long.

This is not true.

A Run-On sentence is a sentence that could be as short as four words. In fact, Run-On sentences have nothing to do with sentence length:

He ran, she walked.
Or:
He ran she walked.

A Run-On sentence is when you put together two complete sentences using only a comma, or no comma at all—and without using any of the seven words (*and, but, or, for, nor, so* and *yet*) to connect the two sentences—as in the examples above.

A Run-On sentence can also be long:

I was telling him yesterday that he's really doing a great job learning all of this stuff about commas, he's just going to keep getting better with practice.

Here's one way to fix this Run-On:

*I was telling him yesterday that he's really doing a great job learning all of this stuff about commas, **and** he's just going to keep getting better with practice.*

Here's another example of a Run-On:

I hated it, I ate it.
Or
I hated it I ate it.

The sentence could be written correctly in a variety of ways:

I hated it, but I ate it.
Or:
I hated it. I ate it.
Or:
I hated it; I ate it.
Or:

I hated it —I ate it.

We'll discuss how to use dashes (—) and colons (:) and semi-colons (;) next, in Part Two.

Learning the commas outlined in this book is the key to avoiding Run-On sentences. Once you've learned these commas, you'll never write a Run-On sentence again.

Unless you want to. Many published writers use Run-On sentences today for effect, despite the fact that they've been considered errors for a long time. These writers are creating a certain effect, by intentionally violating the rule. It is often used in fiction and other creative styles of writing. But in order to do this successfully, you have to know what the rule is and how it works.

Knowing how commas are used can open you up to the possibility of writing very long sentences that are entirely correct. In fact, a sentence, punctuated correctly, can be as long as you want it to be.

Chapter Five
The Comma of Attribution

This is used for quotations. Whenever a speaker, writer or other source is mentioned, a comma goes before the quote, and after the quote if the sentence continues beyond the quotation.

He said, "Get out of my way."
According to the Post, *"Gun violence is on the rise."*
"Get a life," my uncle Roberto always says.
My mama always told me, "Son, marry a nice girl, and settle down," and I will.
"The earth is round," he said, "except where it is flat."

Note: the word "that" can be used when paraphrasing, which means to report what was said without using a word-for-word quote. In these cases, a comma is not used before "that":

The ancient Greeks wrote, "All matter is flux."
The ancient Greeks wrote that all matter is flux.

I told him, "You are a jackass."
I told him that he was a jackass.

Note: You can also leave out the word "that" in the above sentence and other sentences like it:

I told him he was a jackass.

Chapter Six

Commas for Dates and Places

Always put commas between city and state and after state if the sentence continues:
We went to Paris, Texas, for a really fun weekend.

Use commas to separate days of the week from dates and dates from years and years from whatever follows:
I got married on Friday, September 18, 2015, in Campinas, São Paulo, Brazil.

Use commas to separate lines in an address:
He lives at Pennsylvania Avenue NW, Washington, DC 20006, until further notice.

Chapter Seven

What Comma Is That?

EXERCISE 1:

Identify which comma(s) is/are being used in the following sentences:

1.) Comma of Direct Address

2.) Stepping-Away and Stepping-Back Commas

3.) Introductory Comma

4.) Comma of Equal Weight

5.) Comma of Attribution

6.) Commas for Dates and Places

There may be more than one different kind of comma in each sentence.

With Stepping-Away and Stepping-Back Commas make sure to identify both. In some cases, you might find that before stepping back, you will have stepped away multiple times:

Example: *Cats,* [AWAY] *which have fleas,* [AWAY] *as we know,* [AWAY] *though with some exception,* [BACK] *are understood,* [AWAY] *by some,* [BACK] *to be great pets.*

1.) Dogs have fleas, and cats don't ever have them.

2.) We have to figure out if the dogs, which have fleas, are healthy.

3.) Finding a good man to dance with, she spends the rest of the night with him.

4.) I dashed into the station, but the train was late.

5.) "Hi, Jake," I said.

6.) The man on the bus, incidentally, was happy.

7.) He went home to Athens, Georgia, and stayed there.

8.) If wise, a man will drink orange juice.

9.) After today, July 3rd, 2016, there will be no more chocolate.

10.) I like apples and, generally speaking, apples are green.

11.) I like apples, and, generally speaking, apples are green.

12.) Harry, I like apples and, generally speaking, apples are tasty.

13.) A basketball player, if he's any good, will know how to steal.

14.) What is surprisingly easy, however, and we all do it, is to read and understand something but be unable, despite all the best intentions in the world, to correct it in our own work.

15.) As the story goes, when he inexplicably cheated on her with her best friend, they had supposedly been in love for years.

16.) My parents disowned me, for having a baby out of wedlock was unacceptable.

17.) My parents disowned me for having a baby out of wedlock, and I hate them.

18.) He took out his books, finished his coffee, and sat down to work.

19.) What, Jean-Paul, are you doing with your part of the winnings?

20.) However, you try to convince him.

21.) However you try to convince him, he's not going to follow you into that dark alley.

22.) Your name, which is so boring, is going to be famous.

23.) Kris, who is the world most attractive bowler, is also my girlfriend.

24.) Kris, who is the world's most attractive bowler?

25.) Kris, I am happy to say, is about to be my wife.

EXERCISE 2:

In Exercise 2, some of the sentences will contain errors. Identify first whether the sentence is correct or not:

If it is **correct**, as in Exercise 1, identify which comma(s) is/are being used

If it is **incorrect**, correct the sentence, identifying which commas you have used to correct the sentence, or explain why you have chosen to delete commas.

Examples:

The first time I saw her, breathing wasn't so easy. **CORRECT. INTRODUCTORY COMMA.**

The first time I saw her breathing it wasn't so easy. **INCORRECT.**

Correct version: *The first time I saw her breathing, it wasn't so easy.*

INTRODUCTORY COMMA

People, who do not like meat, are vegetarian. **INCORRECT, NO COMMAS ARE NECESSARY**

Correct version: *People who do not like meat are vegetarian.*

Explanation for why commas are removed: Not all people are vegetarian, and not all people dislike meat.

Again, here are the six commas:

1.) Comma of Direct Address

2.) Stepping-Away and Stepping-Back Commas

3.) Introductory Comma

4.) Comma of Equal Weight

5.) Comma of Attribution

6.) Commas for Dates and Places

Here, too, there may be more than one different kind of comma in each sentence.

With Stepping-Away and Stepping-Back Commas make sure to identify both.

1.) If you want to join me.

2.) If you want to join me join me.

3.) Join me if you want to join me.

4.) A good man, is hard to find.

5.) "A good man," Flannery says, "is hard to find."

6.) Finding a good man is a hard thing to do.

7.) Finding a good man to dance with she then spends the rest of the night with him, never doubting her decision never looking for another man.

8.) Finding a good man to dance with, she then spends the rest of the night with him, never doubting her decision, never looking for another man.

9.) Finding a good man is hard to do and I am on a mission to do exactly that.

10.) Finding a good man you know is hard to do and I am on a mission to do so.

11.) Finding a good man is a hard thing to do, but I'm going to do it.

12.) Even though finding a good man is hard, I'm going to do it.

13.) Roses are red. And violets generally speaking are blue.

14.) Roses are red, and like I said, violets are blue.

15.) Roses are red. And violets, like I said, are blue.

16.) I like apples and, like I said, in my technically limited but nonetheless 20 years' worth of experience apples are red.

17.) Roses are red, and, generally speaking, violets are blue.

18.) Roses are red and violets are blue.

19.) She says she met the man whose snake bit her.

20.) She says she met the man, whose snake bit her.

21.) Every time, it happens.

22.) Every time it happens I scream.

23.) Every time it happens, I scream, "Ice cream!"

24.) This story is about a young girl who no matter how feisty and quick she is still knows how important family is.

25.) I got into bed and after a long time thinking about nothing in particular I fell asleep.

26.) Once you were late, there was nothing we could do to save him.

27.) Once, you were late, there was nothing we could do to save him.

28.) Once, you were late and there was nothing we could do to save him.

29.) Once, you were late and, there was nothing we could do to save him.

30.) Once, you were late, and there was nothing we could do to save him.

31.) She went to hell. But, it wasn't that hot.

32.) She went to hell, but it wasn't that hot.

33.) She went to hell. But because of a strange malfunctioning of one of the main heaters, it wasn't that hot.

34.) She went to hell. But, because of a strange malfunctioning of one of the main heaters, it wasn't that hot.

35.) She went to hell. But, it wasn't that hot.

36.) She went to hell. But, strangely it wasn't that hot.

37.) She went to hell. But, strangely, her first day there happened to be a gorgeous afternoon with cool breezes, live music and a welcoming party.

38.) When you get up in the morning and you feel like hell and the first cup of coffee doesn't help you need to reconsider late nights at your friend Tony's.

 39.) Your, boring name is going to be famous.

40.) We are in great danger, but if we swim like crazy, we might not drown.

41.) We are in great danger but, if we swim like crazy, we might not drown.

42.) We are in great danger, but if we swim like crazy we might not drown.

43.) We are in great danger, but, if we swim like crazy, we might not drown.

44.) Howard you are an idiot, but I like you.

45.) However, you are an idiot, so I don't like you.

46.) However much of an idiot you are, Howard, I like you.

47.) You are an idiot Howard however you cut it.

48.) However you cut it.

49.) Sammy I told you not to go but you went, which wasn't a good idea fool.

50.) This, is a complete sentence.

EXERCISE 3:

In the following paragraph, identify any commas that are definitely errors (in other words, not optional). If the comma is correct, identify it.

Again, here are the six commas:

1.) Comma of Direct Address
2.) Stepping-Away and Stepping-Back Commas
3.) Introductory Comma
4.) Comma of Equal Weight
5.) Comma of Attribution
6.) Commas for Dates and Places

When I returned to my old school, I found that the janitor, Samuel Feathers, who at the time had seemed to me to be the oldest man in the world, was still working there. The strangest thing about old Sam was that he recognized me immediately, without hesitation. "Hello, Jason," he said in the same old, angry, rasping voice I remember so well from the times that he caught me sneaking in under the broken chain-link fence to use the piano in the basement underneath the gym. "If you're looking for that old piano," said Sam, "you're too late. It was removed last month by the City because it was seen to be hazardous, so they just took it away. Anything that old should be removed." I said, jokingly, "Then take me!" I immediately thought of you and those terrible sounds you used to make when no one else could hear them except for me. Please tell me that you are not a professional musician or that you're actually a ghost come back to haunt poor old Sam." I couldn't bear to tell him that I was the new school janitor who had come to replace him.

Part Two: Other Punctuation

Chapter One
The Dash

The Dash can be substituted for any and all punctuation:

When I returned to my old school—I found that the janitor—Samuel Feathers—who at the time had seemed to me to be the oldest man in the world—was still working there—the strangest thing about old Sam was that he recognized me immediately—without hesitation—"Hello— Jason" he said in the same old—angry—rasping voice I remember so well from the times that he caught me sneaking in under the broken chain-link fence to use the piano in the basement underneath the gym—"I'll never forget the way you swaggered around here like the king of the school, treating everyone like jerks"—said Sam—"If you're looking for that old piano—you're too late—it was removed last month by the City because it was seen to be hazardous—so they just took it away—anything that old should be removed—" I said—jokingly—"Then take me!" I immediately thought of you and those terrible sounds you used to make when no one else could hear them except for me—Please tell me that you are not a professional musician or that you're actually a ghost come back to haunt poor old Sam—" I couldn't bear to tell him that I was the new school janitor who had come to replace him.

But you wouldn't want to do this. Technically, this is not incorrect, but it might eventually annoy your reader.

Used selectively, it might look like this:

When I returned to my old school, I found that the janitor, Samuel Feathers—who at the time had seemed to me to be the oldest man in the world—was still working there. The strangest thing about old Sam was that he recognized me immediately—without hesitation. "Hello, Jason," he said in the same old, angry, rasping voice I remember so well from the times that he caught me sneaking in under the broken chain-link fence to use the piano in the basement underneath the gym—"I'll never forget the way you swaggered around here like the king of the school, treating everyone like jerks," said Sam. "If you're looking for that old piano, you're too late. It was removed last month by the City because it was seen to be hazardous—so they just took it away. Anything that old should be removed," I said, jokingly—"Then take me!" I immediately thought of you and those terrible sounds you used to make when no one else could hear them except for me. Please tell me that you are not a professional musician or that you're actually a ghost come back to haunt poor old Sam." I couldn't bear to tell him that I was the new school janitor who had come to replace him.

The Dash is most often used to Step Away.

If you use a Dash to step away, you must also use a Dash to step back, unless you end the sentence with a period:

He said hello to his twin who, strangely, looked nothing like him.
He said hello to his twin who—strangely—looked nothing like him.
He said hello to his twin—who didn't look like him.

Note that if you replace commas with dashes, it gives greater weight or emphasis to the material in between.

The Dash is frequently used to join two complete sentences.

The train came in. It was green.
The train came in, and it was green.
The train came in—it was green.

Note: By using the Dash, you avoid creating a Run-On.

The Dash also enables you to step away for a complete sentence. This is something that only Dashes and Parentheses can do:

"Yeah, sure," he said, accepting the drink—Johnny was incapable of turning down anything free—and adding, "Man, I'm not doing well."

The Dash can also be used to replace Introductory Commas—with the same effect of added emphasis:

Yes, I am going.

Yes—I am going.

The Dash can also be used to imitate interruption:

"If you don't stop, I'll—"

"You'll what?"

No answer came.

This is often used in creative writing, such as novels and screenplays.

EXERCISE 1:

Punctuate the following, using dashes or commas. Explain your choice:

1.) When I entered the room she was watching TV and I noticed to my surprise that she was wearing my jeans and they looked good on her.

2.) Jessica is a fool but I like her anyway especially when she lends me money and I don't have to pay her back at least not for several weeks.

3.) All of the best players Jordan Johnson and Bryant started playing before they could even walk as strange as this may sound.

4.) I only just caught the train it was bright green and there were no seats available.

5.) Wow I can't believe this she's dating *him*.

Chapter Two

The Hyphen

A Nashville-born guitarist—if he doesn't have a band—won't have to go too far to find one.

Hyphens are not dashes. As you can see from the sentence above, they are much shorter.

1.

Compound Adjectives

A hyphen is used for Compound Adjectives, to combine more than one word into one larger adjective.

The brown-haired man
The brown-haired, thick-skinned man
The 19-year-old student

If you separate each of the words making up the Compound Adjective, you will see that they cannot work alone to describe the noun. Is the man *brown?* Is the man *haired?* No, he's *brown-haired.*

Not all of the words that make up the Compound Adjective are adjectives on their own.

Rob was a well-intentioned thief.

The word "well" is an adverb, and the word "intentioned" is a verb.

Try this one:

She gave me the I-can't-believe-you're-doing-this-to-me-now look.

Again, you can't give someone an "I" look or a "believe" look. All of the words work together to define the look.

In some cases, two words alone—despite being separate—are so recognizable together that they do not use hyphens when working together as a Compound Adjective. A typical example of this would be a name being used as an adjective:

He had a Mission Impossible *taste in movies.*
The United States is a North American country.

However, when used with other words to form a larger Compound Adjective, hyphens are used between each word:

He had a Mission-Impossible-*meets*-Dumb-and-Dumber *taste in movies.*
Costa Rica is a non-North-American country.

Note: Adverbs that end in -ly are not hyphenated:

The perfectly executed plan
The openly gay football player
The badly dressed actor

EXERCISE 1:

Punctuate the following using hyphens:

1.) These store bought crackers have a very cookie like taste.

2.) The Elvis impersonating villain destroyed the poorly gathered evidence.

3.) She was a bright eyed, boldly dressed, half crazy and eager to please waitress.

4.) A half awake man emerged from the bathroom cleanly shaven.

5.) The compelling mystery book was a half understood masterpiece.

6.) The home built rocket reached into the bright blue sky.
(Note: Was the sky bright *and* blue, or are we defining a shade of blue?)

2.

Compound Verbs

A hyphen is also used for Compound Verbs, to combine more than one word into one larger verb.

She half-opened her eyes.
Are you nickel-and-diming me?
He had over-reached himself.
She double-bitch-slapped him.

3.

Compound Nouns

A hyphen is also sometimes used for Compound Nouns, to combine more than one word into one larger noun. Unlike Compound Adjectives, it's not always easy to determine whether to use hyphens between nouns that form a familiar pair.
Most do not use hyphens: *bathroom cleaner, store owner, disc jockey.*

A few do: *Do-gooder, co-author, X-ray, break-in, self-esteem*

It is also necessary in order to avoid confusion:

Large animal lovers

Are the animal-lovers large, or do they love large animals?

If it's the first one, it should be:

Large animal-lovers

Try this one:

Small bird feeder

Do you mean that the bird feeder is small? Or that it feeds small birds? If it's the bird feeder that's small, it should be:

Small bird-feeder

Just as with Compound Adjectives and Verbs, Compound Nouns can include more than two words:

sister-in-law, Mr.-Know-It-All, jack-in-the-box, good-for-nothing

Language is always changing. Some Compound Adjectives, Nouns and Verbs are in the process of losing their hyphens.

Here are some that you might see in either of these forms:

Co-worker
Coworker

Secondhand
Second-hand

Preexisting
Pre-existing

Run-down
Rundown

Antihero
Anti-hero

Speed-read
Speedread

Pre-owned
Preowned

4.

Compound Adjectives after Verbs

If we move a Compound Adjective to after the verb—without the noun it describes—**in many cases** no hyphens are used.

The half-eaten apple was almost tasty.
The almost-tasty apple was half eaten.

Many of these deal with time, numbers and measurements:

The hour was half over.
The half-eaten apple was almost finished.
The almost-finished apple tasted twice as bad.

When a plural noun is used as an adjective, it is always used in the singular.
The twelve-year-old boy was indeed twelve years old.
The plural noun, "years," becomes "year" when it is used as part of a Compound Adjective.

(This is also true with nouns used as non-compound-adjectives.
The students' gym was more commonly known as the student gym.)

They dug a two-mile-wide channel.
The channel is two miles wide.
(Note where "mile" is singular as an adjective.)

Many sentences similar to those above (where compound adjectives are moved to after the verb) do not involve time, numbers or measurements. These often deal with Compound Adjectives of more than two words:

The man was eager to please.
The eager-to-please man was hard to find.
The hard-to-find man was actually dead.

However, there are **many** exceptions to what we have been describing, where compound adjectives after verbs (not attached to nouns) do not use hyphens. Here are some:

The sky was grey-blue.
My mother is thick-skinned.
My friend is dark-haired.
That loser is at least well-intentioned.
The gift was heaven-sent.

Note that most of these Compound Adjectives can never be written without hyphens, no matter where they show up in the sentence.

EXERCISE 2:
Punctuate the following using hyphens:

1.) A ten gallon hat does not hold ten gallons.

2.) His deal was one in a million.

3.) The three time winner had won three times.

4.) The ten foot well was ten feet deep.

5.) The well placed shot was well timed.

6.) I have always thought of the first time president as well intentioned.

7.) The multi storied house is four stories high.

8.) His aunt can be soft hearted.

9.) All of the dogs were flea infested.

10.) Her I can't believe you're doing this to me now look clearly said, *I can't believe you're being such a jerk.*

5.

Take a look at these:

a.) *19-year-old Quincy wants to be a lawyer.*
b.) *Quincy is 19 years old.*
c.) *Quincy is a 19-year-old.*
d.) *Quincy is a 19-year-old student.*

a.) This is a typical Compound Adjective, as explained in the first section above.

b.) In this case, because we moved the Compound Adjective to after the verb, no hyphens are used. (Note that "year" has been made plural.)

c.) Here, "19-year-old" is a Compound Noun.

d.) This is a typical Compound Adjective, as explained in the first section above.

Chapter Three

Parentheses

Parentheses are used to Step Away and Step Back.

He was watching the game on television (Giants vs. Broncos) when he realized that his girlfriend was no longer sitting next to him on the sofa. (Had she ever been there, or was it just his imagination?) He stood up unsteadily (which was no surprise considering the number of beers he'd consumed) and groped his way to the telephone. This sudden activity (it was a total, terrible shock to his system) caused him to remember that Cheryl had broken up with him. "Cheryl?" he said into the telephone when a woman's voice answered (he was so drunk he failed to recognize the voice on the other end), "Darling, I want you back. Don't listen to your ugly old witch of a mother." "I am Cheryl's mother!"

Parentheses enable you to Step Away and Step Back for:

1.) Incomplete sentences, words and phrases
2.) Complete, separate sentences.
3.) Complete sentences within a sentence (as mentioned before, this is something that only Dashes and Parentheses can do).

(Unlike commas and dashes, with parentheses you must always Step Back.)

Take a look again at the above paragraph. Identify which of the three kinds of parentheses are being used.

EXERCISE 1:

Write a paragraph using each of the three different types of parentheses at least once.

Chapter Four

The Apostrophe

1.

Apostrophes are used to show something has been cut out from within one word or between two words (or more). This is called a Contraction.

I am going. I'm going.

Danielle is ready for tonight. Danielle's ready for tonight.

Felipe will pick her up at her apartment. Felipe'll pick her up at her apartment.

You are not invited. You're not invited.

What are you saying? What're you saying?

We are saying we do not want you there. We're saying we don't want you there.

Where did you get that bitch? Where'd you get that bitch?

We would have done it. We'd've done it.

You all are kidding, right? Y'all're kidding, right?

All right. 'T. (A'ight.)

Here's what can happen if you don't put the apostrophe in:

I know that shed like it.

Is that what you mean? Does this sentence have something to do with a shed?

EXERCISE 1:

See how many Contractions you can make out of the following paragraph:

You are not going to believe me, Danielle is saying. I met this guy, and he is very nice to me—

probably because I have told him at least three times that he is a great guy. "I cannot be a great guy," he told me. "You must not say that. I will be very upset if you say that again. I have done too many bad things in my life, and you would not like me if you knew the details. I know what you are thinking: What is this guy all about, and why is he telling me this?" I do not know why, Danielle continues, but I am crazy about him!

2.

Apostrophes are also used to show Possession, by adding an Apostrophe and an "s."

the king's royal napkin
Italy's vineyards
a clown's laugh
my mother's cooking
men's sneakers
the fish's scales
Chris' bicycle
his sister's book
his sisters' book

If a word already ends in "s," you only need to add an apostrophe.

Other languages do not use Apostrophes to show Possession:

In Spanish, you might write: *El sonido del miao del gato de Enrique.*

In English, this would literally be: *The sound of the meow of the cat of Enrique.*

How would you write this using Apostrophes?

One of the most common errors when it comes to apostrophes is when Possession is confused with Contraction. Here are some words that are commonly confused:

It's and its
You're and your
They're and their (and there)

(Note: *There* is not possessive, nor is it a contraction.)

Most confusion over apostrophes has to do with Pronouns.

A Pronoun is a word such as *he, she, it, you, they, them, him* and *her* that can be used in place of a noun, often to avoid repeating the same noun over and over again.

*When the **king** entered, the court bowed to him, and **he** bowed back.*
*The first time I went to **Italy**, I liked **it**.*
*The thing about a **clown** is you often can't tell whether **it**'s a **he** or a **she**.*
*His **mother** said **she** thought **she** was a clown in a past life.*
*Dear **Mother**, I love **you**.*

Pronouns that are part of Contractions **always** use Apostrophes.

You're, he's, we'd, they'll, I'm, she'd

Pronouns that are Possessive **never** use Apostrophes.

Your, his, our, their, my, hers

EXERCISE 2:

See if you can spot the errors in the following. One of these sentences is correct:

1.) You're on your own.

2.) Its the same color as its eyes.

3.) Your here, and they're over they're.

EXERCISE 3:

Correct the following sentences by identifying, if necessary, where the apostrophe should or shouldn't be.

1.) Ydris favorite thing to do in the morning is to yawn loudly and then flex his muscles.

2.) The boys were the leading gymnasts in the city—some say their "secret powers" had to do with the boys flexibility.

3.) They don't know if they are going. If they are'nt going to be there, then what'll we do?

4.) You didn't know Franks got a girlfriend.

5.) That book has always been her's—she loaned it to Phillip for years, but it was definitely her's.

6.) The police officers arrested the culprit as he tried to climb a pole. The officer's were sweating, and their sweat—the officer's sweat—was a testament to how hard they were working to arrest her.

7.) How many of you think that Kevins' height is what makes him so attractive to women?

8.) Samantha's former gardener didn't steal from her. It was her rich boyfriend, in fact.

9.) Is she or isnt' she?

10.) Starved for attention, Henri's cat meows incessantly all night. Henri's cats' meow isn't the most wonderful thing youve ever heard.

Chapter Five

Quotation Marks

1.

Quotation marks must be used when copying another source word for word.

Danielle said, "I'm not coming out tonight."
According to Shakespeare, the question is, "To be or not to be."
"There's a porpoise close behind us, and he's treading on my tail," writes Lewis Carroll.

If you don't copy down what someone is saying word for word, quotation marks are not used:

Danielle said she isn't coming out tonight.

2.

Quotation marks can be used for dialogue.

"I'm not coming out tonight."
"What? You've got to be kidding!"

In some instances, creative writers don't use quotation marks to indicate dialogue.

3.

Quotation marks must be used to indicate the title of a short story, chapter, article or any other part of a larger work. (The larger work itself requires italics.)

"I Am Born," the opening chapter of Charles Dickens' novel, *David Copperfield*, introduces the narrator.

"There's a porpoise close behind us, and he's treading on my tail," writes Lewis Carroll in "The Mock Turtle's Song."

I read an article in *The New Orleans Times-Picayune* called "How to Make Gumbo," and I ended up feeding it to my neighbor's cat.

4.

Quotation marks can also be used to raise suspicion about a word or phrase—in other words, to question whether or not it should be taken at face value.

His so-called success was all a fantasy.
His "success" was all a fantasy.

The guy she calls her uncle is named Cleve.
Her "uncle" is named Cleve.

The kids love banging around on pots and pans.
Their "music" is delightful.

Sometimes you see this misused:

"Fresh" spaghetti available today!

Did you mean the spaghetti is actually several days old?

Some words have alternate meanings. Quotation marks can be used to favor the alternate meaning:

Danielle says she is "coming out" tonight.

Are you "seeing" her, or aren't you?

I liked her photo, so I "liked" it on her profile page.

In both of the above cases, italics could be used in place of the quotation marks:

Danielle says she is *coming out* tonight.

Are you *seeing* her, or aren't you?

I liked her photo, so I *liked* it on her profile page.

5.

Single quotation marks are used when a quotation occurs within a quotation:

Danielle said, "I'm not 'coming out' tonight."

I read an article in *The New Orleans Times-Picayune* called "How to Pronounce the Word 'Picayune.' "

In his play, *The Cocktail Hour*, Mohinder Shah quotes Krishnamurti when a character says, "My favorite philosopher said, 'All living beings are connected by one thing: energy.' "

6.

Double quotation marks are used when a quotation appears within a quotation within a quotation:

He said, "I read an article in *The New Orleans Times-Picayune* called 'How to Pronounce the Word "Picayune." ' "

And so on, alternating single and double quotation marks as needed.

Chapter Six

The Semi-Colon

1.

The Semi-Colon can be used to separate items in a list:

I bought cucumbers, cookies, coffee, and a copy of the Lagos Times.
I bought cucumbers; cookies; coffee; a copy of the Lagos Times.

The pitcher used a curveball; a sinker; a fastball; a slider.

We have water, soda, energy drinks, coffee or tea.
We have water; soda; energy drinks; coffee; tea.

The "and" or "or" is no longer needed in a list separated by semi-colons, even before the final item.

2.

The Semi-Colon is used to avoid confusion inside lists:

I bought cucumbers, which I needed for the salad; cookies, which were for my brother; coffee, for my uncle; and a copy of the Lagos Times, *for me.*

The pitcher used a curveball; a sinker, his best pitch; a fastball, which reached 100 mph; and a slider, used to strike out the batter.

Here, the "and" helps to avoid confusion.

We have water, bottled or tap; soda; energy drinks; coffee; tea.

3.

The most common use of the Semi-Colon is to combine complete sentences.

What is a complete sentence?

As we wrote in Chapter Three (of Part One), some are short:

I laughed.
Mercy always cried.
The young student yawned for all to see.

Some are longer:

On Friday the student with the highest grades in the class was honored for her ground-breaking paper on the use of the Stepping-Away and Stepping-Back Comma.

These are **not** complete sentences:

Although I laughed
Even if Mercy always cried
After the young student yawned for all to see
Because on Friday the student with the highest grades in the class was honored for her ground-breaking paper on the use of the Stepping-Away and Stepping-Back Comma

Why are they not complete sentences?

This is because using a word or phrase like "when," "although," or "after" creates an incomplete sentence.

Examples of such words or phrases used to begin incomplete sentences include:

although, as, as soon as, because, before, by the time, despite, even if, even though, every time, if, in case, in the event that, just in case, now that, once, only if, since, the first time, though, unless, until, whenever, whereas, whether or not, while.

These are words that in Chapter Three (of Part One) led to Introductory Commas:

Although I laughed, Mercy cried.
Even if Mercy always cried, she was overall a pretty happy person.

Suppose you wanted to write the same sentence without using "although." That would give you two complete sentences:

I laughed. The student cried.

What if you wanted to join them?

A lot of people write:

I laughed, the student cried.

But this is incorrect.

As suggested in Chapter Four (of Part One), if you use a Comma of Equal Weight, this **must always** be followed by one of these seven words: *and, but, or, for, nor, so* or *yet*

You could also choose to keep them as separate sentences:
I laughed. The student cried.

The Semi-Colon suggests a closer relationship between sentences than a period does.

I laughed; the student cried.

The Semi-Colon requires **complete** sentences on **both** sides of the Semi-Colon:

Here are some common errors:

They hung out at the beach; until the sun went down.

The first part of the sentence, "They hung out at the beach" is a complete sentence and could stand alone. "Until the sun went down" is not, so you cannot use the Semi-Colon to join them.

The following, however, **would** work:

They hung out at the beach; eventually, the sun went down.

Both are complete sentences that could stand on their own.

Here are more examples:

His favorite thing to do after school involved the television, and he watched it for six hours straight.

His favorite thing to do after school involved the television; he watched it for six hours straight.

He fed the dog, so it licked his hand.
He fed the dog; it licked his hand.

She didn't want to go to war. She doesn't like fighting.
She didn't want to go to war; she doesn't like fighting.

EXERCISE 1:

Re-write the following using semi-colons:

1.) The student went to the game, and really enjoyed it.

2.) He recognized his girlfriend, who was supposed to be studying.

3.) When his mother came in, he pretended to be studying.

4.) Jeremiah really likes his girlfriend. He is going to buy her a book on grammar.

5.) He knew her brother because he went to school with him.

Chapter Seven

The Colon

1.

The Colon can be used to introduce a list:

When you go to sea, you need the following: a good map, a compass and a picture of a bad-tempered whale.

This is what I told her: I don't love you, I'm not going to marry you, and I left my red pants in your closet.

2.

The Colon can be used to introduce a word, phrase or sentence that completes what the sentences begins to say:

He threw open the door and saw: a dead body on the floor.
That's what she was: exhausted.
That's what she was: a girl with a mysterious past.
That's what she was: she had become a monster.

Here's an example of how a colon can be used to answer a question:

What was his motive? He was deeply jealous of her.
This was his motive: he was deeply jealous of her.

A colon can be compared to other kinds of punctuation in the following way: a period separates; a semi-colon shows a closer relationship; a colon opens a window.

EXERCISE 1:

Write five sentences using colons.

Chapter Eight

Dot, Dot, Dot...

A "..." performs two completely different functions:

1.

"..." is used to indicate that the speaker, or the writer, has left a sentence unfinished:

"I found myself rather dis..."
"Satisfied?"
"No, I mean..."
"Distressed?"
"No..."
"Spit it out!"
"If you'd only let me...finish my sentence, I might..." He trailed away.

Do we need another...
Exercise? No.

2.

The other use of '...' is to tell the reader that some material has been omitted.

Here the '...' helps to cut to the chase.

Example:

The author said in the interview, "Hollywood movies are becoming more and more obsessed with violence. I've always thought so. Links between violent films and increases in urban violence have been shown by many studies."

The author said in the interview, "Hollywood movies are becoming more and more obsessed with violence…. Links between violent films and increases in urban violence have been shown by many studies."

Here's another one:

In his letter of November 17th, 1792, Wordsworth wrote, "I can't stand the way Coleridge bites his fingernails. Before I forget, please ask Betty to get some more plover's eggs. Coleridge is a man it is impossible not to admire, aside from his fingernails."

Wordsworth's view of Coleridge was not always sympathetic. In his letters he wrote: "I can't stand the way Coleridge bites his fingernails…. Coleridge is a man it is impossible not to admire, aside from his fingernails."

EXERCISE 1:

Imagine you're an editor for a newspaper reporting on the president's recent trip. You type up what you have recorded from the interview. It looks like this:

The president said, "On that subject can I have one of those no not those the other ones what was I saying oh yes when I was in Acapulco isn't that what you were asking about I went deep-sea fishing um I found that fishing for these big sea creatures was like the most wait a minute this isn't what I was drinking before uh it is ok the most humiliating boring and unnecessary activity in which I have ever taken part."

Make the president presidential by using the "…" to get rid of anything that wanders off topic.

Appendix

Ten Common Errors

1.) <u>Could of</u> (Should of, Must of, etc.)

INCORRECT: I could of killed him.
CORRECT: *I could have killed him.*
OR: *I could've killed him.*

2.) <u>Her and me</u>

INCORRECT: Her and me went to the park.
INCORRECT: Her and I went to the park.
INCORRECT: Me and her went to the park.
INCORRECT: She and me went to the park.
CORRECT: She and I went to the park.

A good test: Can you say "Her went to the park"?
Can you say "Me went to the park"?

But you can say, "She went to the park."
And you can also say, "I went to the park."

3.) <u>-ing vs -ed</u>

"I am boring," Sam said.
"No, I think you're a pretty interesting guy actually," Emmett said. "I think you mean you're

'bored.' "

"I know I'm an interested guy."

"Hang on. I think you mean 'interesting'. 'Interested' would mean you're interested in other people."

"I don't need a lecture on how to speak from you. I'm tired of your bull."

"There you got it right. You said 'tired.' I am *tiring* you."

"No, you are boring me."

"Thanks, Sam."

4.) d/ed-dropping

INCORRECT: He was a prejudice guy.

CORRECT: He was a prejudice<u>d</u> guy.

INCORRECT: I was upset when he vanish.

CORRECT: I was upset when he vanish<u>ed</u>.

5.) Your vs you're

You're out of your mind.

Your life is your priority.

Your bad habit is the reason you're failing.

6.) There/they're/their

They're over there.

Their books are over there.

There are many students in their school, and they're there, too.

7.) Fewer vs less

As a general rule, "fewer" is used to describe countable nouns. A countable noun has a plural form.

"Less" is used to describe uncountable nouns, which do not have a plural form.

Fewer: books, women, train stations, hours, customers
Less: education, waiting, patience, nature, faith

Fewer books means less expense.
Fewer customers means less waiting.

8.) Then vs than

"Then" is used for time.
"Than" is used for comparison.

Then, he will have more money than me.
He's less good at playing the trumpet than his father is, but then he's only two.

9.) To vs. too

"To" is used as part of a verb (to go, to be, to walk) or as a preposition (to Cleveland, to you).
"Too" is used to say "also" or to suggest an excess.

It's too good to be true.
She's too smart for him, too.
To walk is too much of an effort today.

10.) Lose vs loose

If I continue to lose weight, my clothing will eventually all be too loose.

Alessandro Clemenza

Carey Harrison was born in London to actor parents Rex Harrison and Lilli Palmer, and was brought to America as soon as World War II ended. He has won numerous literary prizes with his novels and his plays, and is Professor of English at the City University of New York. His latest novel is *Who Was That Lady?* Details of his work and life can be found on his Wikipedia site and his website, *careyharrison.net*

John M. Keller is the author of four books of fiction, *A Bald Man With No Hair, Know Your Baker; The Box and the Briefcase, the Moleque and the Old Man and the First Coming of the Second Son of God;* and *Abracadabrantesque.* He has taught writing at the City University of New York, the Universidad de las Américas in Mexico, the Universidad de Montevideo in Uruguay and St. Xavier's College in Mumbai, India. Find him at *knowyourbaker.com.*

Claire Lambe is a visual artist whose works have been exhibited on both sides of the Atlantic; she is a graduate of the National College of Art and Design in Dublin and holds an MFA in painting from the City University of New York at Brooklyn College. For more on Claire's art-work go to *clairelambe.net.*

Acknowledgements:

…Go first and foremost to Dean Donald Hogan, *The Boys' Book of Dinosaurs*, and of course to the groundbreaking work by Jean-Paul Sartre and Albert Camus *Dis, Qui T'as Donné Cette Chienne?*, Editions Gallimard, Paris, 1942, published secretly under the nose of the censors of the Third Reich.

To the memory of my beloved mentor, the distinguished Brazilian educator, Dr. Emanuel Cicero, born in 1907 in Ubatuba, São Paulo. Rector of the College of Rio Grande do Sul from 1943 to 1978, he died in 1988 in Lisbon.

—Maximiliano Reyes, publisher

-FIM-

DR. CICERO BOOKS

26264071R00066

Made in the USA
Middletown, DE
23 November 2015